AN INTERACTIVE
LOOK INSIDE
HUMANS AND ANIMALS

FOLDOUT
ANATOMY

JANA ALBRECHTOVÁ · RADKA PÍRO · LIDA LARINA

BUSHEL
& PECK
BOOKS

Have you ever pondered the diversity of the animal kingdom? So many species, colors, and shapes! The bodies of all animals, including us humans, consist of millions of tiny cells, perfectly organized to make a living individual.

The whole organism never stops working, and each of its parts has to function flawlessly, whether it is a butterfly, a squid, a human being, a snake, or a tiger. To stay alive, every creature must have a solution for things such as eating, breathing, or moving. And, of course, every species must also reproduce—or it will die out.

Would you like to know how it works for different animal species? Leaf through this book, explore each system, and get to know the most fascinating adaptations made by animals.

CONTENTS

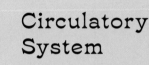

Domestic Pigeon

South American Fur Seal

Pond Slider

Western Lowland Gorilla

SKELETAL SYSTEM

The skeleton is the support frame of the whole body, protecting its organs from damage. Vertebrates such as birds, frogs, snakes, bats, or elephants, and of course humans, have their skeleton inside their bodies.

SKULL
The skull protects the brain. It includes hard jaws used to crush food.

ARM BON

SPINE
The spine enables us to stand upright while also protecting the spinal cord and nerves.

Plains Zebra

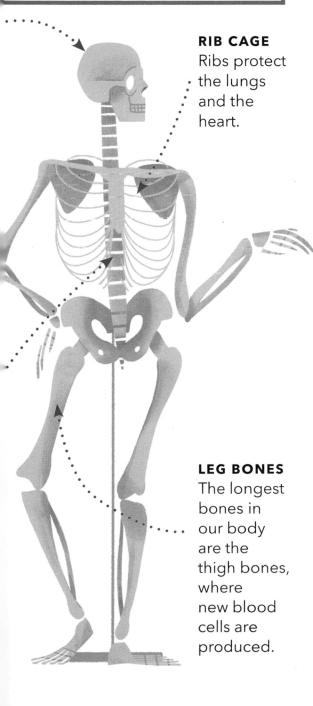

DID YOU KNOW?

The hardest bone of all is the petrous part of the temporal bone, which protects the inner ear. It is also the hardest bone in the body of all mammals.

RIB CAGE
Ribs protect the lungs and the heart.

LEG BONES
The longest bones in our body are the thigh bones, where new blood cells are produced.

Mediterranean Green Crab

Bowhead Whale

Common Noctule Bat

THE MAKING OF A SKELETON

cartilage changing into bone

To begin with, the skeleton is mostly made of cartilage, allowing the bones to grow in length. Later, the cartilage ossifies—it hardens to become proper bone. But cartilage is still present in joints, which enables us to move. Some vertebrates with an endoskeleton (a skeleton inside the body), such as lampreys, sharks, or rays, have a special feature, though. Their skeleton never ossifies, remaining soft cartilage throughout their life.

PROTECTIVE ARMOR

One type of structure is a skeleton on the surface of a body. Critters such as beetles, crustaceans, or scorpions sport a hard shell called the cuticle. However, this surface armor has a drawback. It cannot grow along with its wearer. If the animal wants to grow up, it must take off the old armor and put on a new one.

JUST LIKE JELL-O

Soft-bodied animals such as octopuses, snails, or earthworms do not have a hard skeleton. Their bodies are supported by a small cavity filled with water and surrounded by smooth muscle.

Some animals such as lizards can shed a part of their body. If a little lizard or blindworm is attacked by a predator, it will drop its tail, which continues to wiggle for a while. The lizard takes advantage of the moment of surprise to escape. The predator gets just a tiny snack: a bit of tail.

This trick is possible thanks to the lizard's ability to strangulate vessels between its tail bones. The lizard will later grow a new tail, but its bones will be replaced with soft cartilage. However, a blindworm's tail will never grow back.

HORNS VS. ANTLERS   ↑

The skeleton sometimes includes extensions that protrude from an animal's body. The horns of cattle, goats, and rhinos are rigidly connected to the skull and nourished by blood vessels. The animals cannot get rid of them, and if removed, they will never grow back. But the antlers of red deer and roe deer are a different story. They are made of bone tissue covered in skin, and males shed them every year after fighting for females. New antlers will then grow again from little points called pedicles.

DID YOU KNOW?

Where has our tail gone? A long time ago, all vertebrates had tails. However, the species that had no use for it gradually lost their tail. The human spine ends with the so-called **tailbone**, which is what remains of our distant ancestors' tail.

Common Green Bottle Fly

Great White Shark

Common Noctule Bat

European Perch

MUSCULAR SYSTEM

Muscles enable movement of any kind. Running and swimming, but also breathing and digesting, are only possible thanks to our muscles. Besides muscles, the body also has tendons—ties that connect muscles to bones, allowing the whole body to move.

MUSCLES OF MASTICATION

The muscle usually considered to be the strongest in our body is the one we use for biting and chewing.

DIAPHRAGM

The diaphragm is a breathing muscle, hidden between our chest and stomach. If we irritate it, for instance by drinking soda drinks, we get hiccups.

GLUTEAL MUSCLES

These muscles are the biggest muscles in the human body. We use them not just for sitting, but also for standing up—they control the hip, enabling our upright stance.

DID YOU KNOW?

In vertebrates, muscles make up a third or even half of total body weight.

EYE MUSCLES
The quickest muscle in our body is a tiny one that controls blinking.

PECTORAL MUSCLE

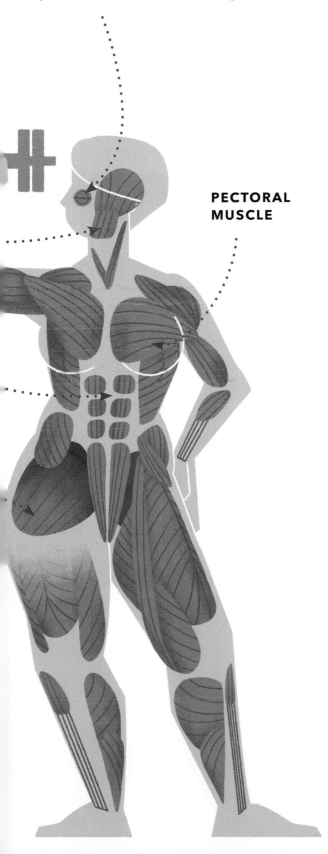

European Herring Gull

Common Death Adder

Hourglass Dolphin

Siamese Crocodile

WHAT TYPES OF MUSCLES DO WE HAVE?

Muscles are divided into groups on a simple principle: whether we can control them or not. Skeletal muscles, as their name suggests, are tied to the skeleton. We can contract and stretch them at will. Smooth muscles work whether we want them to or not, making up the walls of most organs in our body and doing things such as moving food along our digestive system. The cardiac muscle is the heart, which tirelessly pumps our blood.

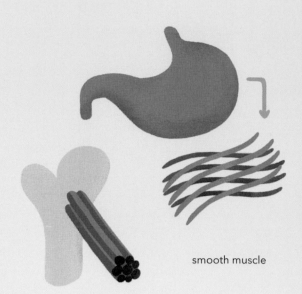

smooth muscle

skeletal muscle

SPEED UP, PLEASE! ↑

Fish and sharks have a quite different muscle layout. It is divided into identical-looking parts. At the dinner table, you may have noticed the huge difference between fish and chicken meat. This fish muscle setup seems to have evolved for living underwater. It explains the typical waving movement that enables the fish or shark to speed up or change direction instantly.

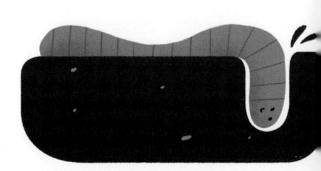

MAKE A FACE! ↓

Mimic muscles, which control the expressions of our face and help us communicate with others, are not distributed equally in the animal kingdom. Only humans and their close relatives, such as chimpanzees, gorillas, or orangutans, can boast such rich facial expressions. Other land vertebrates have much less-developed mimic muscles. And the rest of living creatures? Bad luck. They must communicate in other ways.

STAY WARM ↓

Muscles have one other role besides movement. When we feel cold, they start shaking, producing energy that warms us up a little. In cold weather, this shaking of muscles is an important trick that helps to stabilize the body temperature of all vertebrates—and even some invertebrates.

SOIL TRAVEL ←

Earthworms and leeches move forward thanks to a special set of muscles. A kind of smooth muscle runs in all directions inside an earthworm's body. Their movement using this system is remarkable. First, the earthworm contracts, then stretches in the direction it wants to go—like a yo-yo. Just by stretching and contracting muscles, earthworms push themselves forward through the soil.

DID YOU KNOW?

Single-celled organisms such as protozoans do not have any muscle. They move about using all kinds of flagella. An amoeba moves by shifting its inner organelles and changing shape.

protozoa

Great White Shark

Great Spotted Woodpecker

Four-Toed Hedgehog

European Hare

DIGESTION AND EXCRETION

Eating and digesting is a long and complicated process in humans, starting with the chewing of food in your mouth and usually ending in the toilet. Every living creature must intake food; otherwise, it would not have enough energy to grow and to survive.

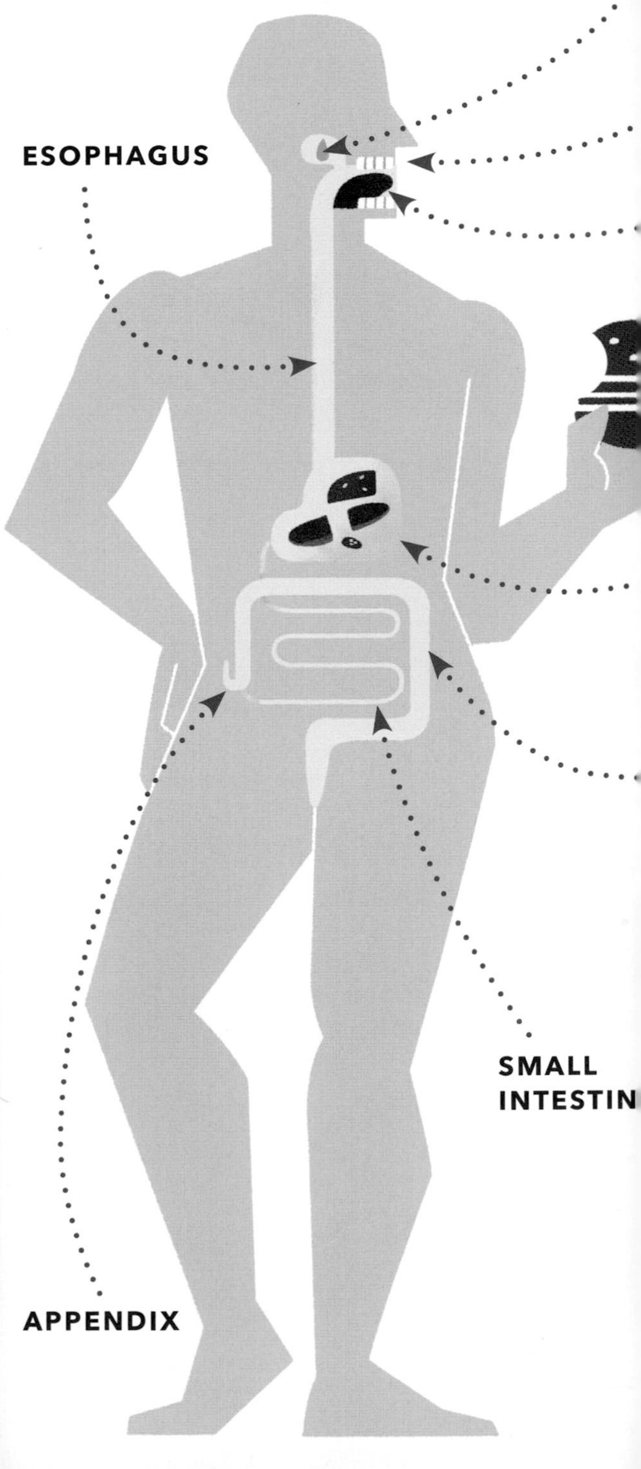

ESOPHAGUS

SMALL INTESTIN

APPENDIX

SALIVARY GLANDS

JAWS AND TEETH
The jaws and teeth tear, chew, and break food into smaller parts.

TONGUE
The tongue tastes food and moves it into the throat. Thanks to the taste buds on its surface, we know right away whether the food in our mouth is good to eat or not.

STOMACH
The stomach produces digestive juices (acids) that help to break down food into small parts that are easy to digest.

LARGE INTESTINE

Domestic Cattle

Siamese Crocodile

Moon Jellyfish

Honey Bee

DID YOU KNOW?

Saliva helps to break down food in your mouth into smaller parts and helps you swallow it. When you have too little water in your body, you are also low on saliva, which makes swallowing difficult.

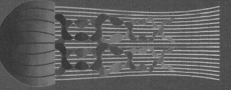

Animals are divided into several groups according to the food they eat. Herbivores eat only plant food. Carnivorous animals like all kinds of meat, but they are not fans of vegetables. There are also omnivorous animals, who like a bit of everything . . . just like humans.

DID YOU KNOW?

Nematodes and tapeworms eat in the simplest way of all; they can do without a digestive system altogether. How? They absorb food across the surface of their body.

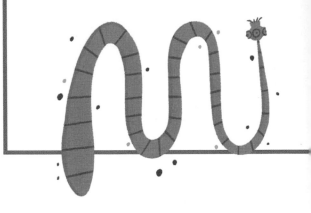

SOME HAVE A MOUTH, OTHERS HAVE A PROBOSCIS

Depending on their favorite food, each group of animals has a different organ at the beginning of their digestive system. Humans have a mouth with teeth, a tongue, and saliva. Gnats have a proboscis to suck blood. Chameleons and some frogs have a projecting tongue to catch insects.

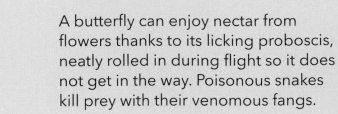

A butterfly can enjoy nectar from flowers thanks to its licking proboscis, neatly rolled in during flight so it does not get in the way. Poisonous snakes kill prey with their venomous fangs.

SHOWING YOUR TEETH ↓

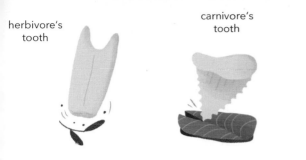

herbivore's tooth

carnivore's tooth

The shape of teeth depends on the type of food each animal eats. Carnivores need incisors to tear meat, whereas herbivores mostly use their robust molars to chew plant food. Some animals grow teeth throughout their lives because their teeth keep rubbing off when they eat. Just think of hares or rodents. Sharks' teeth are replaced with new ones every time they fall out.

WHAT ABOUT THE REST? ↓

While the final part of the human intestine is the rectum, which lets the undigested parts of food out as "poop," other animals such as birds have a different solution. Their digestive system does not end with the rectum but with the "cloaca." The cloaca is also the ending of the excretory system, and often of the reproductive system as well. That is why birds' poop and pee are actually the same thing. You may have noticed the white coating on bird poop—that is in fact the pee. The same goes for animals such as turtles, frogs, or snakes.

WHAT HAPPENS IN YOUR BODY ↓

The stomach produces digestive juices that break down food into small parts. The stomach wall is covered with a protective coating that makes sure the organ is not damaged by stomach acids. Food spends most of its time in the intestines, where it is effectively digested. Sugars, fats, proteins, vitamins—anything the body can use—enter your bloodstream through the intestinal walls.

fats and sugars arriving in the bloodstream

There are useful helpers inside the digestive system that are too tiny to be seen—bacteria. Without them, no creature would be able to process food properly and get as much energy as possible from it.

DID YOU KNOW?

There are animals called coelenterates that live in the sea. They have just one opening, both for receiving food and for regorging the undigested scraps. Their digestive cavity is called the **coelenteron**, and you can see it in jellyfish.

Earthworm

Reticulated Giraffe

Giant Pacific Octopus

Black Garden Ant

CIRCULATORY SYSTEM

Blood carries nutrients and oxygen to all parts of the body—something that all living creatures need to stay alive. Blood also removes any waste products. Humans have a closed circulatory system consisting of two loops: pulmonary and systemic.

THE HEART
The heart is the muscle that pumps blood, sending it throughout our bodies and ensuring its circulation.

PULMONARY CIRCULATION
Blood travels from the heart to the lungs, where it picks up oxygen. Then it returns to the heart.

SYSTEMIC CIRCULATION
Oxygenated blood is pumped into the big systemic circulation system. That means it flows to all the other parts of the body, bringing oxygen to where it is needed. After that, blood flows back to the heart to get more oxygen.

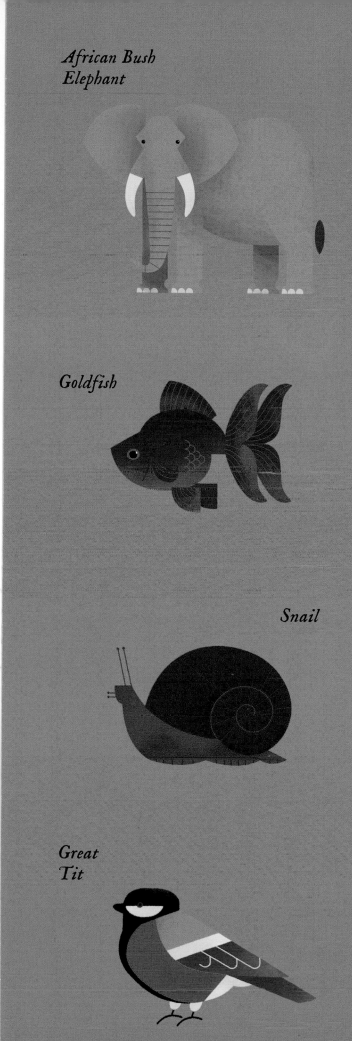

DID YOU KNOW?

Adults have four to six liters of blood in their bodies. The body cannot lose more than a half-liter of blood.

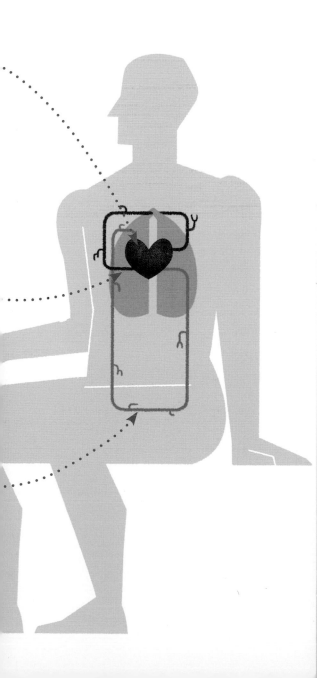

African Bush Elephant

Goldfish

Snail

Great Tit

HOW IT WORKS FOR OTHERS →

Invertebrate animals (those that do not have a spine), such as snails or earthworms, have a liquid called hemolymph instead of blood inside their bodies. Its components are different, but it plays the same role as blood in vertebrates. Invertebrates have an open circulatory system: the hemolymph spills freely everywhere in the body so that the organs and tissues bathe in it, receiving oxygen and nutrients directly. Insects have a different system: they receive oxygen through tiny tubes called tracheae that send it straight to their tissues.

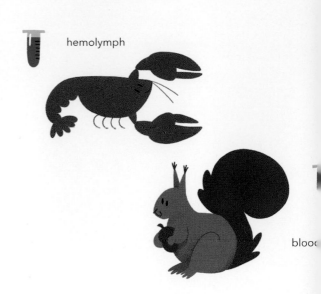

hemolymph

blood

All vertebrates—birds, reptiles, and mammals—have a closed circulatory system. It looks like a huge network of bigger and smaller vessels through which blood flows. This blood flow is ensured by the heart—a pump able to send blood throughout the body.

HOW BLOOD TRAVELS ↓

The blood vessels that bring oxygenated blood from the heart to the body tissue are called arteries. The vessels that transport blood back to the heart are called veins. The veins carry mostly deoxygenated blood, which removes carbon dioxide from our body—it travels to the lungs, and we breathe it out.

HOW THE HEART WORKS

The heart is the most hardworking muscle in the body of vertebrates. No wonder—it can never stop! The heart sucks in blood to send it to the lungs, where it picks up oxygen. The oxygenated blood goes back to the heart to be sent throughout the body, or it flows directly to different parts of the body through blood vessels. This circulation is then repeated all over again.

BLUE OR RED?

The color of blood or hemolymph depends on its contents and the type of protein it has. Hemoglobin is red, iron rich, and the most common blood protein in nature. Hemocyanin is a blue, copper-rich protein typical in mollusks and crustaceans.

DID YOU KNOW?

The biggest heart in the whole animal kingdom is that of the blue whale. This sea mammal is also the largest animal on earth.

A WEIRD SNACK ↓

Besides having lots of functions in the body, blood also serves as food for some creatures. You will surely think of mosquitos or ticks, but there are many others. A bat species that drinks blood is called the vampire bat. There are also some blood thirsty species among fish and birds.

WHAT IS BLOOD MADE OF?

In vertebrates, blood is made of red blood cells that can carry oxygen. It also contains an army of white blood cells that attack all the unknown and dangerous strangers that may cause infection. Platelets help blood to clot when you have a cut or wound.

red
blood cell

white
blood cell

platelet

Blood also cleans the body, removing all the waste products. It transports them to the kidneys, the two bean-shaped organs that catch all waste from blood, expelling it from your body in your urine.

Great White
Shark

Swan Mussel

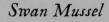

Hooded
Crow

Common Bottlenose
Dolphin

RESPIRATORY SYSTEM

By breathing, you take in vital oxygen and release used air out of your body. The body must get rid of the dangerous carbon dioxide produced during breathing.

TRACHEA
The air travels to the trachea and on to the bronchial tubes, bronchioles, and alveoli.

LUNGS
The lungs are the human breathing organs.

ALVEOLI
Here, oxygen from the air enters your blood.

DID YOU KNOW?

An organ called the epiglottis prevents food from getting into our airways before we swallow it. It is a flap that closes when we swallow. But if we did breathe in some food, it would be a dangerous situation. The body would defend itself by coughing and sneezing.

SINUSES

People inhale (breathe in) through their mouth and nose. The sinuses are areas between the bones in your head where the breathed-in air gets warmed up and cleansed of anything that shouldn't enter the respiratory system.

EPIGLOTTIS

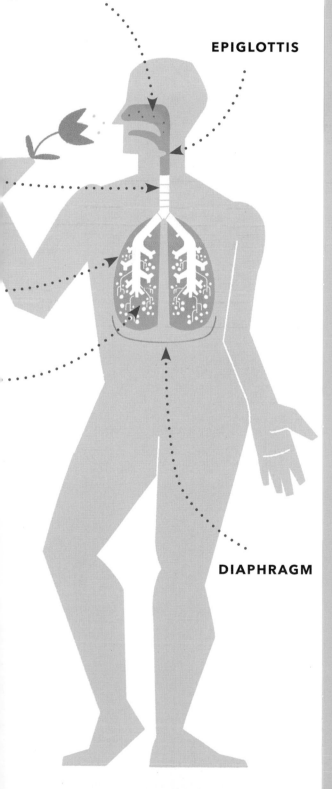

DIAPHRAGM

Horse

Red-Eyed Tree Frog

Common Green Bottle Fly

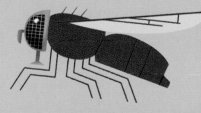

European Perch

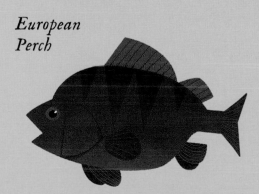

HOW DO YOU BREATHE?

Animals get oxygen into their bodies in various ways. Besides lung breathing, used by humans, there is also gill breathing, skin breathing, or taking in air through body parts other than the mouth.

THROUGH THE SKIN ↓

Skin breathing, or cutaneous respiration, happens across the body surface and is common in invertebrates and amphibians. An earthworm living deep in the soil would not be able to breathe in any other way. That is why it receives the oxygen contained in the soil through its skin. But watch out for rain! It may be a matter of life and death for earthworms. They can only receive oxygen through their body surface when there is some air around them. In heavy rain, they must crawl out above ground, because they might drown in the wet soil.

Frogs can absorb oxygen through their skin both on dry land and underwater. That helps some frog species hibernate deep in the mud of a pool.

USING THE OTHER END ↓

What about absorbing oxygen through the guts or cloaca? That is also possible. Most invertebrates living in water can use an additional breathing system through the walls of their intestines. Even some vertebrates have this ability, for example, a few turtle species. Thus, they can rest underwater for several hours while "breathing" through their cloaca.

DID YOU KNOW?

The bodies of snakes are full of mysteries and fantastic surprises. One of them is the ability to stick their glottis out of their mouth if they want to gulp a mouthful that is too big. That way, snakes can breathe even while swallowing!

BIRD BREATH ↓

The air sacs in birds serve not only as air storage; they also give their body uplift and turn up the volume of their songs.

THE WHALE SPOUT ↓

Looking from a distance at the spouts of whales or dolphins, you can tell what cetacean species it is. The spout is produced when the whale breathes out the humid, warm air from its lungs. When meeting with the colder outside air, this vapor changes into tiny drops of water, and that looks just like a fountain.

IF YOU HAVE NO GILLS

How can you breathe underwater without gills? Humans have designed diving gear . . . and water beetles or insect larvae use a similar trick.

Critters such as the diving bell spider or the diving beetle can take an air bubble with them into the water. The spider has a thick layer of hairs on its abdomen that allow it to take a bubble of air into its web underwater, where it can live happily.

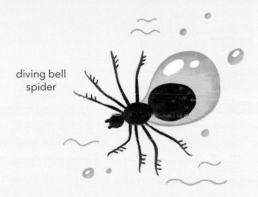

diving bell spider

The diving beetle uses the air bubbles under its wing cases to breathe. Other water beetles even have something like external lungs. Thick hairs on their bodies allow them to absorb oxygen directly from the water.

mosquito larva

Water larvae of various insects use a kind of snorkel—a breathing tube sticking out above the water surface.

Copperband Butterfly Fish

Star-Nosed Mole

Ball Python

Giant Squid

NERVOUS SYSTEM AND SENSES

The nervous and sensory systems play a vital role in any organism—they detect stimuli from the outside world and make sure the body responds properly. The most widespread senses in the animal kingdom are smell, touch, hearing, and sight.

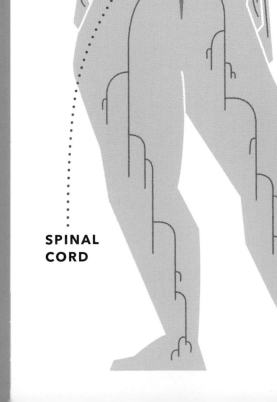

SIGHT
Sight is ensured by the eyes.

SPINAL CORD

BRAIN

The brain is the control center of the body. It is the brain that sends out messages such as that something hurts. The transmission of such messages is ensured by the spinal cord, which runs through the spine, and a dense network of nerves.

HEARING

Sounds travel through the external, middle, and inner ear. Thanks to the vibrations of the eardrum, a membrane inside the inner ear, sound waves are transmitted to the dense network of nerves that lead to the brain.

SMELL

Sensitive receptors in the nose wall pick up scent molecules.

TOUCH

The most sensitive touch spots on the human body are the fingertips.

DID YOU KNOW?

The nerve sensors that receive impulses are called receptors. An organism's response to impulses is called a reflex. Just think how your hand flinches when you touch a hot stove.

Sperm Whale

Painted Lady

Medicinal Leech

Tiger

INSTRUCTIONS FOR THE BODY ↓

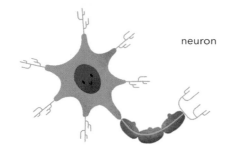

neuron

The nervous system enables us to respond to all kinds of stimuli, triggering an appropriate reaction in our body. Nerve cells called neurons pass all sorts of information throughout the body, such as instructions to move or messages about pain and temperature. How does it work? The neurons send out a signal to, say, a muscle, and the muscle will move.

A MOST DEVELOPED BRAIN ↓

Cnidarian animals such as jellyfish have the most primitive nervous system, which makes their reactions very slow. Critters like insects, crustaceans, centipedes, and earthworms have slightly more complex wiring, but the most intricate among invertebrates is the nervous system of octopuses, giant squid, or cuttlefish; they even have a brain. Vertebrates, however, have the most efficient nervous systems of all animals. In mammals and birds, it has been brought to perfection.

brain of vertebrates

PERFECT ORIENTATION

Each group of animals uses different senses, which means they are not developed equally across all species. Sight is the best orientation tool for birds. Birds of prey such as falcons or eagles will see their prey quite clearly. Even better, they can also guess the animal's distance and speed.

AMAZING HEARING